MW01241203

# What is Happening to America?

## By

## Keith G. Benton

### Copyright, 2015

Also by this Author:

"Married by Faith"

"Do You Know What Is Coming Next?"

Available on Amazon.com

# CONTENTS

**Part 1 - What Is Happening?**

**Part 2 - Isaiah 18: Is This America?**

**Part 3 - Get Ready!**

This book is dedicated

to

The good people

of

Kingman Presbyterian Church

Part 1

# What is Happening?

America has changed radically over the past five decades in character, conscience, and behavior. We who lived through these decades witnessed the acceleration of these changes with alarm. A transformation that began slowly in the 1960s now seems to be progressively gathering speed, and adherents. Those who are younger may not be quite as aware of this drastic transformation, but the America we knew twenty years ago, ten years ago, perhaps only one year ago, is not the America we see today. The standards, morals, and expectations of normalcy in this nation are being ripped away, and many are now welcoming this wrenching revolution.

## Lack of a Standard

Sociologists use the term, "normative force," to describe the general expectation of the vast majority of the citizens in a free society. Any minority that would conduct themselves in such a way as to radically violate or contradict what is considered to be the norm are then ostracized by the majority, and are thus, through social pressure, shaped into the normative image.

Not all allow this shaping to take place, and these make up the small faction of "nonconformists" that are encountered in any group. The behaviors of an even smaller minority that is deemed to be detrimental to the majority is labeled "crime," and the majority arrests and punishes this minority. They may be imprisoned, or even executed.

The changes we are currently witnessing here in America, however, are not so much an evolution of the norm, but rather an absence of any normative force at all. Rather than seeing a societal expectation that might shape standards or conduct, the exact opposite seems to be the case.

In this "New America," any belief or behavior, no matter how radical, is immediately embraced and recognized as legitimate and acceptable. Within this social anarchy, the only thought or belief regarded as intolerable is that which might assume to impose any limits or standards on anyone. Those that dare to suggest the need for such restrictions are branded as "bigots" and "haters," and are accordingly ostracized and punished by the majority. Conversely, those who immediately embrace and endorse any and all aberrant behaviors are lauded as sophisticated and intelligent. In other words, the new "normative force" is a declaration that there is no standard at all. Anything goes!

## How Did This Happen?

This philosophy that is now saturating America is called "humanism." Humanists believe that no religious or spiritual standard is necessary to the formulation of a moral and well regulated civilization. They insist that human intellect and essential goodness can, and does, provide the basis for an ordered society, free of any coercive religious dogma or doctrine. The problem that inevitably arises, however, is recognition of the standard by which intellect and goodness is measured. Who is to say what is good and what is bad?

The wisdom of one group is regarded by others as foolishness, and the resulting arguments sink into a mire of endless debate. Unfortunately, the final solution is just as inevitable as the arguments; all ideas and lifestyles are to be regarded as equally valid and absolutes are to be abandoned. The reasoning goes as follows:

If there is no essential good or evil, as religious doctrine maintains, then there are no absolutes, and all morality and standards become equally valid. It then follows that all behavior becomes acceptable.

Since the basis of acceptance for all these ideas and standards is that human beings are intrinsically good and intellectually capable, then all that is produced by them is the reflection of that goodness and intellect. Thus, there need be no consensus of thinking, but only the absolute demand that any and all ideas and opinions receive unquestioned acceptance.

That demand then inevitably leads to additional demands for more than mere acceptance. Endorsement of the alternative thinking is then required, and any who refuse to agree or withhold their endorsement are, once again, regarded as bigoted and hateful.

## A New Religion: Multiculturalism

The term that has been applied to this new mode of thinking is *multiculturalism*. The "ism" suffix seen here is no error, as it describes a system of belief; actually, a religious dogma. It proposes that all differences between individuals are merely the result of differing cultures. A rich cultural spectrum is very positive, they insist, and no "culture" may be regarded as superior to any other.

It thus follows that no one may attempt to impose their own culture, standard of behavior, or belief system on anyone else. All such attempts are condemned as intrusive and disrespectful, and invite condemnation from the "enlightened" majority.

Such notions as these have their roots in the so-called *Age of Enlightenment* (1650s to 1780s), but humanism became a pervasive influence in America in the late 1940s and 1950s, especially among academics and those in the field of Psychology. The operative term then was "Situational Ethics." University students were indoctrinated in this intellectually arrogant mode of thinking that denied any absolute standard, but instead posited that any given situation dictated what might be considered right or wrong; a corollary of humanism.

The result was the social chaos of the 1960s; the literal explosion of recreational drug use, the rise of "free love," and the collapse of the traditional family.

### America Today

Half a century of time has permitted these seeds to grow to maturity and yield a sad and ugly harvest. Many of the self-possessed rebels of the 1960s are now serving as the professors and politicians that guide our universities and our government, and their loose moral standards have become this new norm; or lack thereof.

Nearly half of the babies born in America today go home with a single mother, and that figure is more like four out of five in the inner cities. Divorce adds to that sum, so that two thirds of the children living in America today will grow up in a single-parent home.

Despite the wealthy and famous that flaunt their single parenthood in the media, these privileged few are far from typical. **The most reliable predictor of poverty** in America is single parenthood, and the most reliable predictor of learning and behavior disorders in children is poverty. If you ever wondered why America has fallen so far behind the other nations of the world in education, you may now see the answer more clearly. These are the children that have been granted a chance at life, though. Many have not.

### A Generation Destroyed

Abortion on demand was institutionalized by the *Roe v. Wade* Supreme Court decision of 1973. Since then, the wholesale slaughter of infants has become a closely held and cherished *right* for the supposedly liberated women of America. And, the total number of casualties is now approaching **60 million!**

We have literally butchered an entire generation of Americans, all for the sake of money and convenience. If a child is not wanted, the pregnancy will end naturally in a matter of a few months, and the child can be put up for adoption. Situational ethics, however, insists that it is cheaper and easier to kill the child than deal with it.

### The Sin of Sodom

That same half century has resulted in a dramatic social revolution in America. It has brought us all the way from the decriminalization of homosexual behavior, to the normalization of homosexuality, to the endorsement of same-sex marriage. Thirty-six of the fifty states passed laws legalizing "gay marriage" before the United States Supreme Court in July of 2015 declared the practice to be a Constitutional right.

The U.S. military in that same time frame went from discharging homosexuals, to a "don't ask, don't tell" policy, to allowing openly homosexual behavior. Military personnel are required to attend "sensitivity training" so they will be prepared to respond appropriately when such relationships are encountered.

These developments have been applauded by advocates of the humanistic philosophy, insisting that the gay lifestyle is merely another part of that spectrum of human culture and expression, never to be criticized or condemned in any way. Those who refuse to endorse the homosexual lifestyle as healthy and normal are, once again, regarded as bigots and haters. The pattern spoken of previously that demands wholehearted endorsement rather than mere acceptance follows here as well. There must be more than an acknowledgement of individual rights.

Those in the gay community now have the right to legally marry same-sex partners, but every victory is followed by new demands. Whoever does not express their joy and extend their blessing at these events must suffer the consequences.

Detractors are being dragged through the courts, sued for discrimination. Some even face criminal charges and fines, charged with Violation of Civil Rights and Hate Crimes for refusing to participate in same-sex weddings.

### God's Law vs. Man's Law?

Since this recent decision by the Supreme Court making same-sex marriage a Constitutional right, new questions have naturally arisen. What of the pastors and churches that will not accept and participate in these same-sex unions? Can these pastors be charged with a "hate crime" for refusing to officiate? Can they be sued for damages?

What of the churches? Can they be legally forced to host same-sex weddings? Can they lose their religious tax-free status if it is determined that they are guilty of discrimination? Once these churches are singled out by the IRS, can they be "taxed out of existence?"

These questions are already under discussion in many circles, and the issue of fundamentalist churches losing their religious tax-free status was actually brought up during the legal arguments before the Justices of the Supreme Court. We are aware as well that a number of mainstream denominations have anticipated just such a legal ruling, and have changed their bylaws to endorse homosexual behavior and same-sex unions.

But, with this redefining of "family," there is the question of the increased numbers of children that will inevitably be living with these same-sex couples. Some are brought in from previous heterosexual relationships, while others are created through artificial insemination or are adopted. What is the result of that experience?

## Normal and Natural?

Many so-called studies have been published that provide assurance of a normal, healthy environment for children being raised in the homes of same-sex couples. Closer examination, however, reveals that the subjects of these "studies" are handpicked. They are anecdotal in nature, utilizing only two or three subjects for evaluation, and have been primarily conducted by organizations that are unquestionably biased towards positive findings.

## Better Evidence

Recent research conducted by Dr. Mark Regnerus at the University of Texas at Austin provides a different picture. In an article published in *Social Science Research* (Vol. 41, Issue 4, July 2012), Dr. Regnerus refuted fifty-nine (59) other such studies as anecdotal and biased. His research revealed the following about the children of same-sex couples as opposed to those living with two biological parents. These children:

- Are four to five times as likely to have received welfare
- Have lower educational attainment
- Have significantly higher incidence of depression
- Have significantly higher incidence of unemployment
- Are four to five times more likely to have been forced to have sex
- Are ten times more likely to have been touched in a sexual way by a parent or other adult caregiver

## History Repeats Itself

As a student of scripture, I am becoming alarmed at the appearance of these specific changes in our American culture and how they seem to mimic the characteristics of an ancient society, the Canaanites. These people occupied the land more recently known as Palestine, and most recently known as Israel. They were driven out and displaced by the Hebrew people, and that forced exit was directed by God.

The Canaanites were immersed in the worship of a false deity called Baal, and the practices of that worship involved three essentials; sexual promiscuity, sexual perversion, and the sacrifice of infants. Temple priests and priestesses served as prostitutes, and also offered the infants to Baal and the various other iterations of that deity throughout the region.

Some worship practices took place in enclosed, wooded areas on hilltops, referred to in the scriptures as "groves" or "high places." Therein, a stone pillar would be erected and the infants would be grasped by the ankles and their brains dashed out against the stone. The bodies were then buried in earthenware jars. Such groves have been excavated by archeologists in modern times, and hundreds of jars containing the skeletons of babies were uncovered.

Another version of Baal called Molech was found among the Ammonites. The idol representing Molech was a great metal creation with a cavity in the belly area. When a fire was kindled inside the idol, that cavity became a red hot oven. Infants to be offered were tossed into the belly of the idol and burned alive. The saying was that the child had "passed through the fire to Molech." (See Leviticus 18:21; II Kings 23:10)

### A Warning to God's People

The Israelites were warned when they entered the land of Canaan that they should drive the inhabitants out. Otherwise, they might be influenced by those that remained. (Deuteronomy 7:1-5)

The Israelites were repeatedly cautioned about disobedience in this matter. They were sternly warned that if they took up these practices themselves; the sexual promiscuity, sexual perversion, and killing of infants, there would be consequences:

*You shall not have intercourse with your neighbor's wife, to be defiled with her. You shall not give any of your offspring to offer them to Molech, nor shall you profane the name of your God; I am the LORD. You shall not lie with a male as one lies with a female; it is an abomination. Also you shall not have intercourse with any animal to be defiled with it, nor shall any woman stand before an animal to mate with it; it is a perversion. Do not defile yourselves by any of these things; for by all these the nations which I am casting out before you have become defiled. For the land has become defiled, therefore I have brought its punishment upon it, so the land has spewed out its inhabitants. But as for you, you are to keep My statutes and My judgments, and shall not do any of these abominations, neither the native, nor the alien who sojourns among you (for the men of the land who have been before you have done all these abominations, and the land has become defiled); so that the land will not spew you out, should you defile it, as it has spewed out the nation which has been before you.*

(Leviticus 18:20-28)

This literal rejection of the people by the polluted land was expressed in the strongest of terms. The NASB version says the land will "spew you out," however the King James translation says that the land "vomiteth out her inhabitants." (Leviticus 18:25 KJV; See also Isaiah 24:4-5; Jeremiah 12:4; Micah 7:13; Romans 8:19-22)

This idea could be expressed by saying that the sins of the people sickened the land, as poison or rotten food sickens the stomach, and the only way to purge out that putrid population was for the land to vomit them out.

Israel did not heed God's warning, and tragedy, poverty, and destruction followed soon thereafter. The Israelites were attacked by the Assyrians, then defeated, captured, and dominated by the Babylonians and the Persians for 70 years before they were permitted to return to their own country. They took up the practices of the Canaanites, and they suffered the consequences.

### A Warning to America?

We have not adopted an ancient religion from the Canaanites, but we have nevertheless come to emulate the practices of that religion. The sexual promiscuity and perversion we now see in America is not conducted by priests and priestesses in some temple, but rather it is promoted and endorsed by the media, the schools, and by many political and religious leaders. No graven image is involved in the murder of millions of unborn babies in America, but we continue the butchery day after day for the sake of a bloodthirsty deity called Convenience.

Let us face the fact: America has become a nation where the practices the Bible reveals to be abominations towards God are not just permitted, but are celebrated. *The America we knew is gone. We are living in Canaan.*

If the land was polluted by these practices, what is America doing to this land we now occupy? Is the time coming quickly when the people of this nation must be vomited out of our land like a sickening poison, just like the Canaanites and the Hebrew people after them?

Some say that the Church in America provides a saving grace that will prevent destruction from coming to us as it did to Israel. The sad contradiction to that notion is the mainline denominations already mentioned that have changed their bylaws to endorse these Baal worship practices for the sake of money, popularity, and social acceptance.

Those that belong to these wealthy, traditional, old line denominations want very badly to be regarded as educated, sophisticated, and intelligent. They want to avoid any connection or association with those that are seen as ignorant bigots and haters. And so, they regard the approval of men to be of greater value than the approval of God. (See John 12:36-43)

## The Destiny of America

Is it too late for America to be saved from its own folly? I never discount God's ability to turn a nation and a people around through the power of His Holy Spirit. Revivals have transformed America in the past, and a revival could deliver us again.

We know quite well, however, that the last days of this present age will be characterized by just the kinds of corruption and vices we are seeing in America now, and that ultimate outcome cannot be changed. We may well be witnessing the events of the end of this age, and of America. The question that often arises, however, is whether or not America is ever specifically spoken of in the scriptures. One particular passage has been the topic of discussion concerning this issue; the 18th chapter of Isaiah. Let us see what this portion of scripture says, and whether it might speak of this nation.

## Part 2

# Isaiah 18: Is This America?

There has been much discussion and controversy concerning the content and meaning of the 18th Chapter of Isaiah. Many believe that it refers prophetically to the United States, while others claim that such an application is fanciful and farfetched.

I have studied the passage, and was intrigued by the possibility that it *may* refer to the United States. This interpretation, if it is valid, is a troubling one however, for the message is not one of hope and blessing but of disaster. The first word of the passage is, "Alas," and that exclamation of sorrow foreshadows the predictions to come.

## Uncertain Identity

One particular feature of the prophecy that suggests that it could possibly refer to this country is the vague identification. Isaiah speaks specifically of many nations in his prophecy; Israel and Judah, Damascus, Samaria, Assyria, Babylon, Moab, Egypt, and others. The 18th Chapter, however, offers only a description of a land with no specific identity. The understanding must be that, although the prophecy refers to a specific nation, the place to which it refers must have been unknown and unnamed in Isaiah's time:

*Alas, oh land of whirring wings which lies beyond the rivers of Cush, which sends envoys by the sea, even in papyrus vessels on the surface of the waters.* (v.1-2)

Could America be described as a land of "whirring wings?" The reference is puzzling, but the application could be to our leadership in aviation. From the Wright brothers on, America has been in the forefront in developing aircraft for both military and commercial use. That leadership has been so significant, in fact, that English is the international language of aviation. Every airport control tower and civil aviation communication network in the world operates in English.

### Envoys in Papyrus Vessels

The reference to "envoys by the sea, even in papyrus vessels on the surface of the waters," is likewise puzzling. When I considered it, though, my first thought was of a book I had read many years ago, an account of a sea voyage by an adventurer named Thor Heyerdahl.

This Scandinavian explorer and scientist became famous for his theory that voyagers from South America sailed across the Pacific to Polynesia, becoming the ancestors of those islanders. He constructed a sailing raft from balsa logs and made the trip successfully just to prove that the voyage was possible, using the techniques and materials available in that ancient culture. His book about that experience, *Kon-Tiki*, was very popular, as was the documentary film that followed.

In later years, DNA tests on the Pacific islanders proved that Heyerdahl was probably right; that their ancestry could be traced to the Americas rather than to Asia as was previously thought.

Not as many, though, are familiar with two later voyages that Heyerdahl made. He sought to prove another theory; that ancient voyagers from the African continent traveled to the Americas and influenced the people there. His evidence for this interaction involved the presence of pyramids in both the African/Egyptian and South American cultures, and also some obscure and unique construction techniques that were found on both continents that are essentially identical.

Once again, Heyerdahl set out to prove his theory by sailing from Africa to the Americas in an Egyptian boat of ancient design. This 45-foot sailing vessel, named the *RA* in honor of the Egyptian sun god, was constructed out of bundles of *papyrus reeds*, a technique used by ancient Egyptians that is carried on even today.

That first vessel, launched in 1969, made most of the voyage successfully, but failed just 600 miles short of its destination. Heyerdahl constructed a second vessel of papyrus reeds the following year, however, the *RA II*, and completed the 4000 mile journey across the Atlantic from Africa to Barbados in just 57 days. The accounts of those voyages can be seen in Heyerdahl's book, *The RA Expeditions*, and the documentary film that followed.

So, was Heyerdahl correct in his theory? Were there envoys traveling back and forth from Africa to the Americas in ancient times, using vessels constructed of papyrus reeds? If so, we see a reference to the American continent that would correlate to the time and the culture of Isaiah's day. This application of the prophecy also explains the reference to this unnamed land lying "<u>beyond</u> the rivers of Cush." The modern name for the region called Cush is Ethiopia in northern Africa, and a land "beyond the rivers of Cush" would be off to the west.

### The Nation, "Tall and Smooth"

Once again, the description of these obscure, unknown people seems a bit puzzling:

*Go, swift messengers to a nation tall and smooth, to a people feared far and wide, a powerful and oppressive nation whose land the rivers divide.* (v. 2)

Why would any people be referred to as "tall and smooth?" Certainly, we know that genetic and nutritional factors in the United States produce almost the tallest average overall height in the entire world. (We are only surpassed slightly by the Scandinavian countries such as Sweden, Norway, the Netherlands, and Iceland due to their more homogenous population.) The reference to the people of this unknown land being "smooth" is a bit more complicated.

The prophecies of Isaiah date to around 720 to 700 B.C. The ancient culture of the Hebrew people was essentially established by Mosaic Law, and the law stated that men were not to cut off the "corners" or "edges" of their beards. In other words, their beards were to be left natural, untrimmed. (Leviticus 19:27; 21:5)

The Greek culture was characterized by trimmed beards, as can be seen in the statuary from that period. The Romans that followed, however, were normally clean shaven. Their military was the first in the world to require soldiers to have close cropped hair and shaven faces, and the fashion of the day was the emulation of that military image. Statues and mosaics of the period provide us with the evidence of a "smooth" population.

American culture is quite a bit more varied. We see fashions of facial hair come and go in the United States, but we are, for the most part, a cleanly shaven people after the Roman fashion; especially since the 20th Century. Therefore, a people "tall and smooth."

That brings us to the next point, which is that this prophecy could not have applied to the United States a hundred years ago. We are not the people or the culture we were in the 18<sup>th</sup> and 19<sup>th</sup> Centuries, and not just in terms of our fashions and appearance. Through a series of amazing and tragic events, we became a worldwide super-power.

### The Sleeping Giant Awakened

The prophecy of Isaiah 18 describes a nation that is "feared far and wide... powerful and oppressive." The United States, in its infancy, was anything but "powerful and oppressive." Washington's Continental Army was able to eke out a victory over the forces of King George, and managed to drive out the English again in the War of 1812. Our own Civil War (1861-1865) was devastating to the entire nation, but proved to be the impetus that caused us to develop the weapons and skills of war to an entirely new level.

Armies that relied upon muzzle loading muskets and primitive cannon at the beginning of the Civil War were using howitzers, repeating rifles, ironclad ships, and multi-barreled machine guns just four years later. We were still primarily an agrarian culture and isolationist in our policies, however, until the early 20<sup>th</sup> Century.

America became involved in the war in Europe in 1917, and there was no turning back. World War II brought the United States to the forefront of global politics, and our highly skilled military, our industrial might, and our development of nuclear weapons in 1945 caused us to suddenly become that nation described in Isaiah 18; "powerful... feared far and wide." We may not see ourselves as "oppressive," but it is undeniable that our presence and influence is felt around the world.

Interesting as well is that time factor as it applies to the "whirring wings" mentioned in verse 1. It has also been within this past century, as we became a world power, that our dominance in aviation developed as well. A century ago, we would not have been a nation "feared far and wide," and, we would also not have been the "land of whirring wings." Now, we are.

### "...Whose Land the Rivers Divide"

Even a casual glance at a topographical map of the United States reveals the great rivers that transect our land. The Mississippi River was both a barrier and an avenue of travel and trade throughout our history, and we tend to identify entire regions of the country by labeling them as "east of the Mississippi" or "west of the Mississippi." The Missouri River was also significant in our history. It was the route taken by Lewis and Clarke in their exploration of the Louisiana Purchase, the frontier of the American West.

Look carefully, and you will begin to see that description emerge. The Ohio, the Tennessee, the Wabash, the Susquehanna, the Mississippi, the Missouri, the Chattahoochee, the Illinois, the Platte, the Arkansas, the Snake, the Yellowstone, the Green, the Columbia, the Brazos, the Pecos, the Canadian, the Red, the Gila, the Colorado, the Sacramento; all the mighty waterways of the United States of America. We are, indeed, a land the rivers divide.

Just one portion of this brief passage still remains unexplained. What are the "swift messengers" of which Isaiah writes, and what is the tragic message they are bringing to this powerful western nation? It is at this point that we begin to understand the beginning of the message, and its use of the tragic warning, "Alas."

## Swift Messengers Are Coming

The Hebrew words translated "swift messengers" are fairly straightforward. The Hebrew translated "swift" means exactly that; even the swiftness of a flash of light. The word translated "messenger" is also literal, meaning one who is *dispatched* to deliver something. It can also mean an angel, or one who has been dispatched by God, but the word used in the Isaiah 18 text is *MAL-AWK'* and is slightly different than the Hebrew *MAL-AK'*, the literal Hebrew word always translated "angel."

The King James translation of the Bible attempts to connect the mention of these "messengers" with the "envoys" mentioned earlier (*TSEER; one who is sent on an errand),* by connecting the phrases with the qualifier, *"saying..."* That word has been added by the translators, though, and is not a part of the Hebrew text. The New American Standard Bible makes no such connection, but allows the mention of "messengers" to stand alone.

The text tells us that these *"swift messengers"* are being sent to this mysterious nation that lies to the west, this unknown land that is "feared far and wide... powerful and oppressive." So, what are the tidings that these *swift messengers* bring?

The scripture describes the proclamation of a war against this nation to the west. The standard and the trumpet spoken of are the signals for the beginning of an attack. What we find to be unusual is the understanding that this proclamation is seen and heard by everyone on the face of the entire earth!

*All you inhabitants of the world and dwellers on the earth, as soon as a standard is raised on the mountains,*

*you will see it, and as soon as the trumpet is blown, you*
*will hear it.* (v. 3)

Skeptics of the accuracy of scripture used to scoff at a passage in Revelation that states that people from all over the world will look upon the bodies of God's two Witnesses as they lie in the streets of Jerusalem during the Great Tribulation. (Revelation 11:1-10) Then, the technological miracles of satellite television and the internet made such instant worldwide observation to be commonplace. In the same way, Isaiah 18 tells us that all the world will watch and listen when this great nation is being attacked.

## Where Will God Be?

The next verse is a quote by Isaiah from the LORD directly:

*For thus the LORD has told me, "I will look from My dwelling place quietly… Like dazzling heat in the sunshine, like a cloud of dew in the heat of harvest.*

(v. 4)

The events that are about to take place are not God's doing. He is "quietly" observing from His "dwelling place," heaven," as these events unfold.

The understanding we get is that what is to follow is not a direct judgment from God, but an event that results from human action. This is not a calamity from heaven, such as we see in Revelation, but rather an event carried out by conventional warfare. But, what is this event that is about to take place?

## The "Swift Messengers"

The prophet writes that "swift messengers," will be dispatched to this nation to the west, this powerful country that inspires fear, far and wide, this land that the rivers divide. Then, as the Lord observes quietly from His dwelling place, He sees the result; "dazzling heat" and "a cloud."

Could there be a more graphic description of intercontinental ballistic missiles than calling them "swift messengers," sent towards this western nation? When we envision the immediate results of a nuclear explosion, the first effect that is seen is searing heat and a blinding flash, "like dazzling heat in the sunshine." What follows immediately is the iconic mushroom-shaped cloud, "like a cloud of dew in the heat of harvest." The prophecy continues:

*For before the harvest, as soon as the bud blossoms and the flower becomes a ripening grape, then He will cut off the sprigs with pruning knives and remove and cut away the spreading branches. They will be left together for mountain birds of prey, and for the beasts of the earth; and the birds of prey will spend the summer feeding on*

*them, and all the beasts of the earth will spend harvest*
*time on them.*                                    (v.5-6)

The words, "before the harvest," are especially significant in this passage. A time of "harvest" is spoken of repeatedly in biblical prophecy.

Matthew 13 contains Jesus' parable of the wheat and the tares. In it, He tells of a landowner who sows good seed. An enemy comes later, however, and sows "tares." (This is a weed that resembles wheat while it is growing, but yields no grain.) When the servants of the landowner tell him of the worthless tares growing with the wheat, they ask if they should go through the fields and root them out. He cautions his servants that the wheat might be uprooted along with the tares, and tells them to allow both to grow together, *"until the harvest,"* when the tares will be gathered into bundles and burned, but the wheat gathered into the barn.

The parable is then explained by Jesus later on to His disciples. He identifies the Sower as "the Son of Man," the good seed as "the sons of the kingdom," the enemy who sowed the tares as "the devil," the tares as "the sons of the evil one," and the ***harvest*** as ***"the end of the age."***

We see further reference made to a "harvest" in Revelation 14 when God's direct judgment upon the earth is described:

*Then I looked, and behold, a white cloud, and sitting on the cloud was one like a son of man, having a golden crown on His head and a sharp sickle in His hand. And another angel came out of the temple, crying out with a loud voice to Him who sat on the cloud, "Put in your sickle and reap, for the hour to reap has come, because the **harvest** of the earth is ripe."*

(Revelation 14:14-15)

The events we see described in Isaiah 18, then, are not a part of the Great Tribulation, God's direct judgment upon the earth, but occur *before the harvest,* or before the end of this present age. God is merely observing as the destruction unfolds through human agency, but takes no action to prevent it.

This event will also occur when this western nation is yet young, *"as soon as the bud blossoms and the flower becomes a ripening grape."* America is still in its ripening period, as nations go. It has been in existence less than 250 years, and its present strength as a world power is less than 100 years old. If America is the nation described in Isaiah 18, however, it will progress no further.

*"Then He will cut off the sprigs with pruning knives and remove and cut away the spreading branches."*

The next portion of the prophecy is even more sobering. It describes utter devastation in which victims of the slaughter will lie on the open ground for months afterwards, unburied, as they are fed upon by birds and wild beasts. (This neglect could be the result of high levels of radiation.)

*They will be left together for mountain birds of prey and for the beasts of the earth; and the birds of prey will spend the summer feeding on them, and all the beasts of the earth will spend harvest time on them.*

## The Cause for the Destruction

The other feature of this prophecy of doom and destruction that appears most strange is that there is no immediate revelation of its cause. Isaiah writes of a powerful and oppressive nation, feared far and wide, but we do not understand immediately why it is attacked, nor why God simply watches. What could this great and mighty nation have done to deserve such devastation? Then the revelation comes:

*At that time a gift of homage will be brought to the LORD of hosts from a people tall and smooth, even from a people feared far and wide, a powerful and oppressive nation, whose land the rivers divide – To the place of the name of the LORD of hosts, even Mount Zion.* (v.7)

The "gift of homage" spoken of here comes from the Hebrew *SHAH'EE,* meaning simply a gift. The root of this word, however, is *SHAW VAW',* meaning to *equalize* or *adjust.* Thus, it is translated as "a gift of homage."

The term, "homage," comes from feudal times. It refers to a gift brought by a vassal to his overlord, a tribute offered to express reverence and respect. This gift is brought, it seems, as *repentance* for previous disregard or lack of respect for this *"place of the name of the LORD of hosts... Mount Zion."*

That place is Israel, and we may now understand why this great and mighty nation is to be punished.

### The Ancient Covenant

If Isaiah 18 does, indeed, describe present day America, we must be concerned at the development of current events regarding our relationship with the nation of Israel. The people of God's choosing, the descendants of Jacob, have been restored to their own land through a miraculous series of events. The prophetic scriptures that predict Israel's restoration have been fulfilled, and we have yet another indication that we may be approaching the end of this present Age of Grace. Those same scriptures warn us:

*Now the LORD said to Abram, "Go forth from your country, and from your relatives and from your father's house, to the land which I will show you; and I will make you a great nation, and I will bless you, and make your name great; and so you shall be a blessing; AND I WILL BLESS THOSE WHO BLESS YOU, AND THE ONE WHO CURSES YOU I WILL CURSE. And in you all the families of the earth will be blessed."* (Genesis 12:1-3)

Whether or not the prophecy of Isaiah 18 pertains to the United States, we must at least heed the warning of Genesis 12. We are seeing the administration currently in power slowly but surely turning away from the nation of Israel.

When the Prime Minister of Israel, Benjamin Netanyahu, visited Washington in the spring of 2015 to address Congress, the President refused to meet with him or even be present at his congressional address.

Soon after, we witnessed the signing of a nuclear arms deal with Iran, a nation that has sworn to "wipe Israel off the map." These openly bellicose threats were utterly ignored during the negotiations, however, by our representatives and those of several other world powers.

## A Nation Accursed

If the United States turns against its longtime ally, Israel, we will be calling upon ourselves the curse of Genesis 12 and, in so doing, stepping out from under the Lord's hand of blessing and protection. Israel surely will survive without us. But, can we survive without Israel?

Isaiah 18 might *not* pertain to the United States, despite all the evidence. But, if this passage does pertain to the U.S., we can take comfort in only one thing... that there will still be enough left of our country after its devastation that we will be able to belatedly repent for our great error. Isaiah 18 tells us that this unnamed country, this "people feared far and wide, a powerful and oppressive nation, whose land the rivers divide," will afterwards offer respect to the people of Israel. They will present a "gift of homage" to Zion.

What does all this mean to the individual believer in Christ, though? What can we do right now? Part 3 will provide the answer.

## Part 3

# Get Ready!

While we, as individual believers, cannot change the policies of a nation, we can still function effectively as the living, working body of Christ in this present world, and that is exactly what we must do now.

In my study of biblical prophecy, I have discerned one great truth over and over again; The Bible does not equip us to predict events to come, only to prepare for them. We are told that no man knows the day or the hour of the Lord's return; not even the Son, but the Father only. (See Matthew 24:36) I can assure you that if *Jesus* doesn't know the day or the hour that He will return, neither do we! Setting dates for the fulfillment of biblical prophecies is absurd.

At the same time, we find that Jesus was critical of those that did not recognize the signs that indicated the fulfillment of prophecies that were actually taking place all around them during His ministry. (See Matthew 16:1-3; Luke 12:54-56)

We are also told to be aware, always on the alert, for the events around us. We are to be continually ready for the Lord's return. (See Matthew 24:37-42; 25:1-13; Luke 12:35-48; 21:27-31) These scriptures speak of more than just anticipation, though. They tell us of the tasks the Lord has left for us to do, and of the necessity that we be busy carrying out those tasks. There will be tough circumstances to overcome, though.

## Difficult Times Ahead

The scriptures make it very, very clear that we are not going to be just blithely skipping along in a perfect and ideal world when, suddenly, *WHOOSH!* We are all raptured out of here. No, instead we are told that world events are going to get progressively worse and worse as this present age draws to a close, like the progress of labor pains for an expectant mother. Jesus described a time of wars and rumors of wars, earthquakes, famine, severe epidemics, treachery and betrayal, false prophets, and persecution. (See Matthew 24:1-13) We are told as well, though:

*This gospel of the kingdom shall be preached in the whole world as a testimony to all the nations, and then the end will come.*                    (Matthew 24:14)

In the midst of all this chaos and suffering, the Church finishes strong. We are equipped for and capable of carrying out all that our Lord has given us to do.

Be aware, though, that this proclamation of the gospel of the kingdom, this worldwide testimony, will not be accomplished by a bunch of Crybabies, spending their time criticizing and complaining instead of studying and praying!

The kingdom of God is not just in word, Paul tells us, but in *power.* (I Corinthians 4:20) The Church needs to get filled up with the word of God and the power of the Holy Spirit now if we are going to be up to the task at the end of this age. That is why we need to *GET READY!*

## Tough Messages from America's Pulpits

Faith comes by hearing, and hearing by the word of God (Romans 10:17). That fact alone places a lot of responsibility on the leadership of our churches. The time is long past for "nice" Sunday sermons that lull us to sleep... physically, mentally, and spiritually. Messages straight from God's word are sometimes tough to hear, but necessary if the Church is to be prepared.

As this age draws to a close, situations are going to get desperate, and people are going to get desperate. They are going to have many needs and many questions, and we must be ready to meet those needs and answer those questions.

It will also be a time when earthly resources run out. The Lord will become our *source,* but we need to hear the message of faith and begin depending on Him as our resource *now!*

There is an old story about a man whose roof was leaky, but he never fixed it. When it was leaking, there was always a storm going on. Then, when the storm was over, he didn't need to fix the roof!

This is the situation in much of the Church today. When times are bad, people cry and complain, but find faith to be too difficult under such circumstances. Then, when times are good, they forget all about God and start relying on their earthly resources again.

If we wait until things get desperate in the closing days of this present age, it may be too late. We have to start now. We have to respond in faith and live according to the promises in God's word *now!*

Tithing is a good beginning. If we can trust the Lord to pour out a blessing on us as we are faithful in our finances, our confidence will shift from the natural to the supernatural. (See Malachi 3:10) The Lord becomes our source of assurance rather than a fatter bank account.

We have to become prepared for the tough times ahead. The scriptures point out to us over and over again that our treasury should be in heaven, and that worry and concern about earthly things profits nothing. (See Matthew 6:1-4; 25-34; Luke 6:38; I Timothy 6:17-19) We need to *GET READY!*

## The Supernatural Church

Paul told Timothy that, in the last days, difficult times would come. He described the character flaws that would be common in people, and we know he was talking about those who claimed to be Christians too! He ended that description by saying that these selfish, mercenary, pleasure-seekers would still retain "a form of godliness," but would "deny its *power.*" He told Timothy to avoid these folks; turn away. (See II Timothy 3:1-5)

Thus, we understand what will divide the church at the end of this age; the crisis issue. Some will hold firmly to the message of power. They will preach deliverance from sin and its consequences. They will continue to call upon the great Healer and Provider. They will lean upon the God of Peace when the world no longer offers any peace.

Others will drift further and further away from the gospel and be overcome by popularity, power, and corrupt desires. They observe a mere form of godliness, religion and its trappings, but forget about God's power to save, heal, and deliver. And, these two factions will continue to drift further and further apart as the day of the Lord approaches.

## Where Will You Stand?

Where will you stand as the day of the Lord comes ever closer? Which direction will you take? If you drift with the current, if you go in the direction that most of America is going now, you will end up very far away from Christ's body and the power that is needed to deal with the world situation at the end of this age.

The time for playing church is over. We are seeing the signs fulfilled all around us that we are the generation that will see the end of this Age. I tell you, *GET READY!*

*******

If you have further questions about biblical prophecy and the events of the end of this Age, you will find the answers in the Author's book:

*"Do You Know What Is Coming Next?"*

**By**

**Keith G. Benton**

Available at Amazon.com

Made in the USA
Middletown, DE
13 October 2023

40507480R00024